The Sharp End of the Stick

An Attempt to Solve ~~...~~ *Problems by an O...*

The Sharp End of the Stick

*An Attempt to Solve America's Problems
by an Ordinary Man*

JOHN A. BALDWIN

iUniverse, Inc.
New York   Bloomington

The Sharp End of the Stick
An Attempt to Solve America's
Problems by an Ordinary Man

iUniverse books may be ordered through booksellers or by contacting:

iUniverse
1663 Liberty Drive
Bloomington, IN 47403
www.iuniverse.com
1-800-Authors (1-800-288-4677)

ISBN: 978-1-4401-4974-0 (pbk)
ISBN: 978-1-4401-4973-3 (ebk)

Printed in the United States of America

iUniverse rev. date: 9/2/2009

Preface

I must admit that writing *The Sharp End of the Stick* has proven very challenging and even draining for me. Never having been in a position that required much actual written words of me, this experience has given me a new understanding and respect for authors everywhere. I also have to mention that, without the support of my wife, this book would not have been possible. People say things like that all the time, but what I really mean is, *thanks for not killing me, dear!* Because of my perseverance, my determination, and my way of doing things, she may have been thinking that she wished she had!

I sat down at our home computer one day back in early February 2008, frustrated with life in general. I thought maybe if I made some notes to myself about what was bothering me, it would help me feel better. Thirty-six hours later, I went to bed. I found myself (a two-finger typist) unable to stop writing, and I wasn't even writing what's in this book.

It was a list of events and grievances compiled from over the past few years of my life, about all the different ways I had been taken advantage of. As I started reviewing what I had written, I realized that people, at least the people I had been dealing with, had lost what I would call any "real dignity." I thought, *How could these people be so heartless and treat others this way?*

Well, as my wife can tell you I don't quit easily, so I was on a personal quest to satisfy my curiosity and heal myself. Along the way, I realized that Americans everywhere were dealing with a lot of the same problems. Each time I spoke with friends or family members, inevitably they would ask what I was up to. When I would tell them, each one would say, "Oh, you should include this or that on your list also." The list just got longer and was in no particular order. Soon I had so much to say that I decided this would be *an attempt to solve America's problems by an ordinary man*—me. I was going to put my manuscript on the coffee table in our home for any visitor to read. But after a long tug of war with myself, mostly from a big fear of rejection, I decided I had something to say to America. I give you these observations, my opinions, and my solutions; I hope Americans will find something among the many topics they can relate to, and we can find the answers together.

Introduction

In the United States of America today, *We the People* have become a bunch of finger-pointing whiners! People find it easy to blame others for almost any shortcomings they may have or that they may be feeling, whether it be pertaining to their own lives or to the world around them. It seems people just wait to pounce on anyone who appears to be better off than they are or who has different views from them. For sometime now, the people of this country have just sat back and witnessed the American traditions and values fade away. We have no one to blame but ourselves. Worst of all, most of us are not willing to step up and make real changes.

Harsh words to choke down? Yes, but these words

were never truer, as the United States goes through some of the most turbulent times in our history. Our economy is in the toilet. Crime is running wild all around us. Unemployment is on the rise. Americans need change, and we need it now! Furthermore, it must come from all of us—not just a select few.

What has happened to the American spirit? Are American values truly gone? Where has the American workforce gone? Are we hiding from the truth? Why are we having such stressful times? These and many much tougher questions are on my mind daily and for good reason. As I see it, the problem is that none of our so-called leaders have any good answers for the American people.

In 2008, an election year here in the United States, America was facing one of the worst economic times in decades. It would be easy to just throw up our hands and blame all of the turmoil on the Bush administration, or on any of the past administrations for that matter, but would that truly be an accurate assessment? I think not.

Let me start here by saying that I am one of the thousands of Americans who has lost his job recently. At first, I was really quite upset over losing my job and looked to blame someone or something. Was it poor management, lousy decision making at the top, or poor planning? Sure, that was all part of it. Anyone with half a brain could tell that all of that was true—at least that's how it seemed to me. The changes in my life and my view of a very troubled America had sparked my curiosity. I wanted—no, I needed—to know why these events were happening, and not just to me.

During that time, as the months passed, I found

myself focusing harder and harder on the hardships and troubling events taking place in my life as well as all the turmoil I saw happening in this great country of ours. I began taking things so seriously that I felt the weight of America's troubles on my shoulders. I felt a responsibility to find the answers for myself as well as for the American public. The ensuing stress I put on myself was eating me up inside. I became increasingly more irritable. While most of my friends and family could see my stress, I could not. I was blind to it.

My health was on the same downward spiral as was my attitude. In tandem, both were plummeting.

I was dealing as best I could with my personal problems, knowing I wasn't alone and that the rest of the nation was dealing with the same issues as I was. All Americans faced new troubles that came in the form of fluctuating fuel prices, rising food costs, failing financial institutions, and just plan old crooks. News stories kept bombarding my thoughts as hundreds of hardworking people were losing their homes for one reason or another, maybe due to greed or maybe their own poor financial education. Then there was a lack of employment both locally and nationally. All I could see were problems everywhere I looked in the country, and I hated it. I felt helpless, but what could I do? I don't see myself as an expert with special abilities; I'm just an ordinary man.

On top of all the helplessness I felt, I viewed the daily decline on Wall Street as further proof of my concern about the state of affairs in America. Now my life savings, like those of so many others, had been cut in half seemingly overnight.

With all this turbulence around me, I was keenly

aware of the fact that this was an election year and of the candidates in the running for office. Each candidate had long lists of promises but lacked any real answers to the problems we face in America. Listening to these men and women just confirmed my certainty that we were in for more troubles—more BS from the politics that I had come to know and that we Americans just accept in this country.

It occurred to me that maybe I should do something. I should look for solutions or focus on the root causes of the problems in America, at least as I see them—causes or problems that people never ever want to admit to. *Someone had to pick up and use the sharp end of the stick*, I thought to myself, *and this time it might as well be me.*

The more I thought about it, the more I realized that "the sharp end of the stick" was never more necessary than now because, as you are about to read, I'm going to point it where it hurts the most, even though the truth is never easy to hear.

I say aloud, this country has become lazy. We are a nation of people who expect handouts for doing nothing. Like little babies, we throw tantrums. "Give it to me now! I deserve it!" We want it all, but I see that many aren't willing to put in any effort to get it.

Ouch, that hurts! That's not me, is it? You bet it is. To everyone who says that it's not them, I say, *I hope you stop kidding yourself and being so foolish.* The fact is, many of us observe what someone else has—the apparent wealth and abundance and happiness—and most of us want those same things too. Fact is, no one wants to actually work for what they desire, nor wait until they can really afford it. I will be the first to admit I was lazy, greedy, and looking for instant gratification as well. Of course, that doesn't mean it is something that I'm proud of.

Back in 1975, fresh out of high school, I started looking for a secure line of work with a future. In March of 1976, I landed a job with a large electric utility company as a union laborer in a power plant. That's where it all began for me, with my years of turning a blind eye to the fall of America's greatness. Take, take, take, and "never give a sucker an even break!" Not cool, just plain greedy. That is not the way I was raised to think.

My father is the hardest-working man I know, and he is still going strong in his midseventies! Even though I believe my father is a great man, a man who raised me to be the best person I could be, even he was guilty of greed and dishonesty, which is a typical learned behavior, as I would later figure out. My father taught me that "you take a man on his word and his handshake, which is good enough." Dad was also a union worker, for the phone company in the city of Chicago; he has a great amount of pride in himself and everything he does.

If my father gave you his word on something, you could always count on him—period. I like to think you can count on me when I give you my word as well. It just feels right to be honest and dependable, but even that is not enough to overcome temptation or peer pressure in America, as I would soon find for myself.

As a member of a union, I quickly learned that there were more than just the union bylaws to follow. There were the unwritten laws, rules never to be broken. I learned that if you did break the unwritten laws, you were putting the screws to your union brothers and sisters.

I recall my first week on the job; I was given a task

that I found to be very easy. The gentlemen I was working with and I had finished our job assignment in less than two hours. I said to him, "Let's go tell the foreman we're done and see what he wants us to do next."

"Hold it right there," my co-worker said. "We have rules, kid. This job takes four hours. We need to lie low for a few hours until after lunch. Then we can go get a new assignment."

I said to him, "But what will the foreman think?" My co-worker replied, "He knows how long this job takes. He was in the union once himself."

This seemed a little nuts to me. I was puzzled and wondered why would we not go and get a new assignment. Also, why would the foreman, if he already has this knowledge of the job, overlook this? I didn't want to get into any trouble. I was, after all, on a ninety-day probation period. Besides being on probation, I needed the job to support my new family. I was married now, and my wife and I had a child on the way. On the other hand, I didn't want to get the men and women I worked with upset with me. I was the new kid on the block. So I thought about it and caved in and went along with the guy by keeping my mouth shut. I hid out with him for a few hours, feeling like a child who had done something bad. In fact, wasn't that what I was doing?

That's the way it started for me. I hated not doing an honest eight hours of work for eight hours pay, as my father had taught me. I was now on my way down the road of less production for more pay.

Are you shocked? I didn't think so. Most of you reading this have to admit that it would be rather hard to recall when, if ever, you put in a full day's work for a full day's pay. It seems that most Americans want as much as they can get with as little effort as they can put out. Sadly, that's become the American way.

I believe it is this mentality in the United States that has gotten us to where we are today. In this world, there is so much greed and a constant struggle for power or recognition that people are choking to death on it. Somewhere along the way we have forgotten what made this a great country in the first place.

We've become a nation that depends entirely too much on our government or on businessmen and women to find the solutions needed to fix the mess we are in, when, in fact, government and powerful businesses are just as much to blame as the rest of us are for creating these problems, and maybe more so. Let someone else fix it! That's the battle cry in this country at this time, and so nothing changes. We all need to focus on change to make our world a better place.

In my relatively small world, there is a good cross section of Americans, all with many of the same things in common. First off, most of my acquaintances, friends, and family are great at complaining but do nothing to change those complaints. They complain about taxes, fuel cost, government spending, or just not having enough of whatever.

The more I focused my attention and pondered on the complaints, I realized that these acquaintances, me included, were spoiled by the evolution of this country. As men and women the world over created ways to make life easier or faster, people everywhere became more and more complacent. I'll give you an example of what I'm referring to. In the so-called old days, the entire family worked together to keep food on the table, a roof over their heads, and clothes on their backs. They had to, for survival; no one else was going to do these things for them. Also, not so many years ago, if people made purchases on credit, it was their number-one priority to pay their creditors back as soon as possible. They had little things I call pride and self-respect, which compelled them to do the right thing. The opposite is true today, where people typically take longer to repay their debt and think nothing of the interest they accrue in doing so. This practice has pushed a lot of Americans to where they are today, consequently, with a large percentage of households much further in debt than financially advisable.

Americans everywhere have bitten off more then they can chew, as the saying goes, and they are not ready to give anything up to change that fact. Again, I say we have become a society that wants it all and are not willing to wait to get it. Today, in this country, people are losing some of their most prized possessions, like their homes and autos. Yet they still hold on to things like cell phones, cable or satellite television subscriptions, cigarette smoking, or going out for dinner, when they should be cutting back and looking for ways to get out of the financial trouble they've gotten themselves into. In general, credit companies and society have made it easy not to be held responsible, so people feel they are not responsible!

This slow decline in American values and morals has also made it so that employees feel their employers or government owes them more for doing less. American workers steal every day from employers and never give it a second thought. The American way is to waste time at our jobs. We take longer breaks throughout the day, we use company phones to make personal calls, we browse the Internet on company time, we take home company products such as pens, paper, towels, batteries, and so forth—anything people can get their hands on and get away with. This lack of production and thieving is reflected in everything we purchase today. Employers have to increase the cost of their products primarily due to less productivity and losses. This is the current-day American way and the values reflected today. This attitude is wrong, and it doesn't seem like it will ever stop; so, for broader purposes, I will focus on what I feel are the big-picture items.

Only you as an individual can make changes in America, but not until you're ready to admit you may be part of the problem.

Who Gets the Cake and Who Gets to Eat It?

Here is an example of how far we've come in the United States today in resolving a major concern for Americans. The consumption and dependency of oil in America has been a long-standing issue since I was a young man. I personally found this out firsthand back in October of 1973. I recall the shortages back then that forced me to sit idle in mile-long lines, waiting my turn at the pump, and I remember the panic it caused. The long gas lines in those days were just the tip of the iceberg, and we ignored it. That should have been a wake-up call. The Organization of the Petroleum Exporting Companies (OPEC) was holding all the cards, and the lion's share of the world's oil supply, and we should have been looking for ways to change and improve the situation.

Yet, almost forty years later, is the problem any better? No. Actually, it is much worse as many Americans experience a historic rise in fueling their cars. The effects of our dependency on oil to heat our homes, fuel our autos, and run big industries has created a huge headache for America, not to mention the global warming issue that affects all of mankind. Oil burned in America today still pollutes and decays the ozone layers, and all we do is talk about it; few people are taking action to fix it. Isn't it true that the manufactures of oil and oil products experienced their most historic profit margin ever, in 2008? So one could assume the American people did not change, and we still don't commute in the most effective ways possible or change our driving habits. In turn, the demand directly affected the supply; greed and the attitude that someone else will fix it still remain.

I recall back in the 1970s, the auto industries were being pressured to make cleaner-burning cars and trucks. Hence, one solution was to use unleaded fuel. Also, catalytic converters were introduced into the marketplace on new automobiles. Now that may have seemed like a good idea at the time, and indeed it may have been. But I think the question became, *how does big business prosper from all of the new emission constraints?* That's what they were asking themselves: How do we, the government and big business, make this work in our favor?

I laugh to myself when I think about this, because I remember the big oil companies' move was to take the polluting lead out of the gasoline. That actually meant one fewer step in the refinement process, which was to add the lead in the first place. One fewer product added to the fuel should have meant less cost outlay for the company, correct? Oil companies then raised the price of that same gas for the American people.

Today, I ask myself why. Was it really to help the environment? My opinion: no! It was greed—greed of the people in these big businesses to fatten their pockets. Politics as usual—that's how it appears to me. What is in the best interests of government and big business is almost always diametrically opposed to the people's best interests!

The American auto industry then, in turn, rolled out some of the worst gas-guzzlers the world has ever seen. You may have already guessed what came next. Yep, they also raised the price on those automobiles. The ball of pain to the common person just kept rolling on from there (*the sharp end of the stick*).

With the cost of automobiles on the rise and fuel prices fluctuating, American workers must have recognized that the big auto manufacturers and oil industries were getting fat and happy (wealthy) off their labor and innovations. Politicians were also getting what they wanted—a way to get activists and the EPA off their backs—but the American worker didn't see a dime of that profit or become able to breathe cleaner air.

Furthermore, the buying power of the average American's "hard-earned" dollars wasn't going as far as it once did. So, in turn, the people doing the real work demanded their cut of the pie! I remember strikes that threatened American business and workers happening with much frequency back in those days. Even as American workers got their cut, they still didn't increase their productivity; in fact, they started to waste even more time.

The American workers realized that slowing down productivity was a way of getting back at the powers that be. Today, this has become the accepted norm. Employees take time off "sick" when they aren't sick but expect to be paid. People use every excuse they can come up with to be compensated more for doing less. Now, this may be a hard pill to swallow for some of you, but most of us know it to be true if we are being really honest with ourselves.

Union workers are not the only ones guilty of doing this; this runs rampant in almost every workplace in America. Call me what you will, but the truth hurts, doesn't it?

Today, the American auto manufactures (GM and Chrysler) are going bankrupt. They have never been able to compete with the foreign (Japanese) auto companies who took a more serious approach to solving problems the auto industry faced. Who knows if American auto companies, had they taken these and other problems more seriously, we may have been able to avoid this situation? Instead, we, the American taxpayers, will suffer and pay for their greed and lack of concern and innovation.

American Pride:
Part of the Problem or
Part of the Solution?

There are plenty of good, hardworking people who will disagree with what I'm saying here, but to them I ask, *how many have seen these things taking place at your workplace and have chosen to do nothing about it?* So then, if you're not part of the solution, you are part of the problem. If all you do is complain in silence, what good have you done, and how can you expect change for the better? Americans have become a people who say, *Let the other guy worry about it, and it will just go away. I only need to worry about myself, so the heck with the other person.*

We need to *stop* and smell *the sweet smell of pride once again*. Pride in a job well done. Pride in knowing you are part of the solution and not part of the problem. Pride! It's become such a rare commodity these days. But I know that it is out there somewhere and yearns to be found. We as Americans need to re-ignite the flames of innovation once again and work together to find solutions to the complex problems we face today in this country.

We can no longer allow the mentality of "let someone else fix it" to pollute our way of thinking. Americans need to stop saying "I can't do anything about it" and to start asking ourselves "How can we do something about it?" I, for one, refuse to stop beating this drum.

It won't be easy—change never is. But if we just take it one step at a time, one challenge at a time, and all get together and pull or push in the same direction, we can accomplish anything. That's what I firmly believe.

The very idea of a free ride to successfully repairing the problems we face in this country is a joke. Our government wastes so much time and money on some of the most ridiculous things, it would make your head spin if you knew the half of it. Let's get that money re-deployed to do some real good. We give unemployment money, food stamps, and free medical care to thousands who don't deserve it, while people in real need get left out. People's lives are tied up in the political red tape of government foolishness, and this in turn only confirms people's thoughts of corruption and greed by the powers that be. I have heard statements firsthand by many men and women, such as *why should I go look for work when the government owes me this free money?* Or *why should I take that job? It's beneath my dignity, and besides, I get more on unemployment.* Or *He* [or she] *gets to live off the government, so why don't I do the same?* Keep up this way of thinking, and we will surely fail and become a second-rate country very soon.

You know that first impression you get of someone before you even get to meet him or her? Most of us form an opinion at that moment based on appearance only. How would you, as an outsider looking in at Americans, see them at first sight? You would not have such a good opinion, I would wager. But we can change that if we all take action now.

There are so many countries around the world getting financial aid, food, and military help or support from the United States, yet the world at large still views us Americans in a bad light. I say, *let's stop wasting time with them and repair the damage we have done right here at home.* That's not to say that we are not needed in other parts of the world, because we are, but shouldn't we be helping our own countrymen first?

To those who would say we don't need a military presence in other parts of the world, I say, *get real, people!* We do need to protect our interests as well as our allies in other parts of the world. Or to those who whine about their sons and daughters in the armed forces being killed in far off-lands for a cause they don't believe in, here's a news flash: we don't have a draft in this country last time I looked!

These brave men and women all enlisted knowing it was the military they were going into and that there would be danger and the real possibility of loss of life.

I have tremendous respect for each and every one of the brave men and women in the armed forces, but

I can't stand by and choke down the drum beating of the so-called do-gooders saying it's not our place to be in other countries! America, we should not complain about helping people in other parts of the world, like Iraq, that are ruled by evil—regardless of whether or not we found stockpiles of weapons of mass destruction! We did find a people longing for help after having been brutally murdered and torn apart by a dictator who was so evil it's much too hard for any of us to imagine. The need to help others is great, but we need to pay as much attention as well as to our own people. That's all I'm saying.

America, look no further than in your own backyards, and see how we as Americans are being ripped apart by greed in our homeland right now. Government spending is out of control, and what are you doing about it? Not a darn thing, in most cases—just like many of you would have had our country do in Iraq, which is nothing.

Most of us are great at complaining, when it's action that's really needed! Instead of doing what's easy and safe for you, why not become part of the solution? Do something positive! Stop sniveling and whining, and start working to save this country of ours!

If each one of us did just one good thing to help solve the problems we face here in America, this great land would be a Garden of Eden. Whose responsibility is it if it isn't up to us? Who's going to save the land we all love so much—the politicians? They've had their chance as long as you and I have been alive. How's that going? How's that been working out so far?

The trouble here is that most of us are groomed throughout our lives to sit back and wait and see. See what? See our children and grandchildren suffer in a land that has unheard-of debt and that has been terrorized like never before in history? This is a world filled with sick people bent on corruption and thieves tearing at the souls of the good-natured folks of this country. Every time we catch a corrupt group of politicians or businessmen, for example, other politicians vow to get to the cause of the problem, vowing to protect the good people from getting ripped off or hurt ever again. Too bad those politicians and their committees have fallen short almost every time!

When you need to get something done at your own home, you either take care of it yourself or it doesn't get done, right? What I am saying is that it is time to take care of America. Let's get something done to solve the problems right here at home. The voice of the people crying out to government will help, but not if the politicians just blow off their show of concern or make light of what they are trying to say.

Education

I'm going to cite a few of the problems we Americans are facing today, as I see them, starting with education in America. I firmly believe that we need a total reform of the school systems in the United States. Once again, harsh words, but as I have said before, we're talking about *the sharp end of the stick*! The citizens in this country are way behind the rest of the world when it comes to our education system—when what we really need is to be educating our children at least as well as, if not better than, other countries!

Our children lack the fundamental tools they need to make educated decisions, which they are just not taught in school. As an example, where in our educational system or program do we teach our kids about finance? Hmmm! I can't seem to recall any talks on that subject. That topic has never ever come up in the past thirty-plus years as my wife and I raised our five children. I know this because we helped them with their homework. Finance wasn't taught in school; it was left up to us as parents to teach our children good or bad financial habits, depending on the parent.

Do we have a financial crisis going on in America today? Yes, and it's a big one, believe me this time it's really bad! Why is that, I wonder? I'll tell you, but you can probably see where I'm going with this. It's due to the lack of education on the subject of finance—a subject that should never have been ignored in the first place.

I believe we need to start teaching this subject to our children as soon as possible, as a requirement in the grade schools across America. If you think it's not a big problem or no big deal and that our kids can pick it up as they go or that you can teach them what they need to know, you're wrong! Let me show you why.

Let's take a look at the meltdown we are facing in America right now with the housing markets and lending institutions. First and foremost, put greed at the top of your list of causes. Some of the most well-known names in the financial industry flat out blew it as they took advantage of an uneducated America. I need not mention any of these institutions by name, but I will say they did their damage. Most of the brass escaped with a big fat wallet before their companies went belly-up and left thousands of Americans holding the bag.

Not only did thousands of mortgages fail across this land, but also thousands of men and women working for those companies lost their jobs. I believe this was due to greed and the lack of financial education.

America was flying high with financial wealth and freedom through the earlier years of this decade. Low-interest-rate loans were being offered around every corner, allowing previously under qualified borrowers to become qualified borrowers. These soon-to-fail big financial institutions then had to become more competitive to get your business. They came up with creative ideas to help hardworking, educated, and uneducated men and women with new ways to finance their American dreams. What these institutions really did was to help people overextend themselves, which resulted in many devastated lives. People were given loans equating to more debt than they could handle, as these creative institutions got rich. These foolish people were trying to "keep up with the Joneses," as they say. Americans were purchasing bigger homes, fancier cars, and other big-ticket item but, all along, were getting in way over their heads with debt. That's what's been going on here, folks. Let's face it and do something about it.

Many of us go out, and we buy things we can't afford on credit because of what we see around us. Credit was made readily available to anyone with a Social Security number. Qualifying for credit went out the window as the credit card companies relaxed their conditions for qualifying for credit. I recall one of my own children getting in debt way over his head by using credit cards. My son came to me for advice when the credit companies were coming down on him, as he could no longer make the minimum payments.

During our conversation, he stated that I was to

blame for his problems. I could not believe what I was hearing from my own son's mouth—the young man who I thought was educated on such matters. "How do you figure it's my fault?" I asked him.

"Well," he said, "I was raised in a home with a lot of nice things (big-screen television, nice furniture, nice car, a swimming pool), and that's what I've become accustomed to and came to expect for myself. So I went out and bought all those nice things because I deserved them. You can't expect me to live differently than you raised me." Holy cow, I was floored. *Have I really created this monster?* I thought.

I told him, "You're blind, son, and have a very short memory to boot." I then reminded him of his childhood and the sacrifices both his mother and I had made so that our family could eventually have those nice things. We didn't start out with all those things. It took a long time to acquire them, I explained.

For years and years, I drove a piece of junk 1970 Ford Maverick back and forth to work. The car had over two hundred thousand miles on it. It was a rust bucket; the floor was mostly rusted out and gone. If I had not replaced the floor with a piece of plywood, I could have watched the road go by right under my feet as I drove. The windows were wedged closed, or they would have dropped down out of sight. I could not open the driver's door because it too was rusted shut. I had to climb in and out of the passenger side. During the winter, I had to bundle up as warmly as I could, then get in the car and wrap myself in a sleeping bag just to stay warm, because the car had no heat, plus the wind blew through it like the car was a piece of Swiss cheese!

I reminded my son that I had worked every bit of overtime at the power plant just so I could make payments on a dependable car for his mom, brothers, and sisters. "Transporting you kids and your mom around safely was all I cared about," I said. "I didn't worry about myself; it was you I needed to take care of. Everything I have, I've worked hard for," I went on to explain to this misguided soul whom I call my son.

Today, I'm happy to say he's gotten himself out of all of his bad debt and back on his feet. It took him eight years and cost him everything he had purchased as a result of his poor judgment and the greedy financial institutions. I say greedy financial institutions because, after all, they should never have given him the lines of credit that they did.

I do worry about him still today, although he's now in his thirties and was tricked once again and persuaded into buying a modest home with a five-year balloon mortgage on it. He was told, like countless others, that interest rates would remain low and that they could refinance at an even lower rate sometime in the future.

My point here is, even though I thought I had prepared him for his ventures in the real world of finance, there was no way to know how he would be thinking or how he would be influenced by these outside forces. People are just not as educated as they need to be in this rapidly changing world, and that needs to change now!

Do you know that I have spoken with people who think if their investments go down by 50 percent and then come back up 50 percent, that they are back to even? It's true. For those of you who can't see what's wrong with this thinking, look at this: You start out with let's say

$100, and it drops 50 percent. Now it's only $50. Then it comes back up 50 percent, which means it now is only $75. Got it?

So, I say let's start reforming the education system so that we can stop this type of devastating event from ever happening again. Just think of how much emphasis we as a country put on a good college education, not to mention how costly that education has become. Now take a look around at how many college-educated men and women there are in this country who are out of work. They're losing their homes, losing their cars, and they have huge credit card debt they can't handle. This problem is not hard to find; it's everywhere you look. This sends up a red flag to me and screams out that we need to change, and we need to change now! Let's focus on giving our kids the tools they need right now in the twenty-first century, before this lack of education about finance wipes us out.

If we examine what is taught to our children in schools across this great land, I'm certain we will find that it's old and outdated in most cases. I say, let's start teaching children the skills they need to become good, well-informed, productive, and innovative citizens of this great nation once again. "United we stand, divided, we fall," and, people, let me tell you: *we have fallen.* Americans have fallen short, time and time again, and I shouldn't need to say this any more: Stand up and be heard; demand reform. Be a mentor! Do something! We are the United States of America, for crying out loud, so let's get re-United!

I had a good laugh the other day; some of you might like this story. While out in public, I witnessed, firsthand, a young man staring at a clock on the wall of a building for several minutes. I looked on as this guy struggled to read the time. I'm sorry, but that struck me as funny. Why? Because then he pulled out a cell phone from his pocket and played with it some. Then he started looking around like he was totally lost and approached me. "Can I help you?" I asked.

"Yeah," he said. "My cell's dead. Do you know what time it is?" So I told him. Now that's good stuff, right? As if that wasn't bad enough, the reason it was so funny to me was because the clock on the building wall had hands on it instead of a digital readout! I will say one thing in this totally confused person's defense: the clock did have diamond shapes on it instead of the numbers one through twelve … yeah, that had to make it tough on him!

Here's another story I find amusing. A few years back, I went into a major electronics store. My wife and I shopped for about twenty minutes, selecting our items, and then we proceeded to the checkout counter. The salesperson informed us that their computer was down, so he could not make the sale to us. I was dumbfounded by that. "You're going to turn away a sale because your computer is down?" I asked.

"I'm sorry, sir, but there's no way for us to keep the inventory straight if we did the sale."

I asked him, "Whatever happened to the good old pen and paper method for tracking sales?"

"Oh, we can't do that. That would be too hard for us to keep the records straight. Also I could not accept money or make the correct change without the computer," he informed me.

He went on to tell us that there was no way to figure out the price of any items or figure in the tax on them either. I just shook my head and walked out. There must have been twenty or thirty people in that store while we were there, and that's a lot of sales to turn down due to not being able to use a calculator or a pen and paper!

If I ran a business in that manner, it would go broke in no time. The very idea of turning away customers like that is a joke! This only reinforces my opinion that Americans have become a lazy people and attributes to the sorry state of education in this country today. Once again, only my opinion!

Come on, people. We have got to do something about this. Don't just sit there and wait till the government decides it's time for change in the way our children are taught. We need to make the politicians hear our cries for help now. No child left behind, really? Ha! It's time to stop fooling around and to start educating again, with programs that teach real-life, twenty-first-century circumstances, period.

Look, my views are not intended to offend anyone. I make them known merely to get people thinking for themselves instead of letting others think for them. Think; you surely have your own opinions and your own mind—we are all equal in that respect, people. All I'm asking you to do is to think for yourselves, and maybe we can clean up this mess we Americans are in.

I know that teachers across this great land who may be reading this are probably saying *what does he know? I work hard to educate the students in my classes.* I'm sure that they do, for the most part, but it's what the kids are *not* taught that matters to me.

I love to educate, teach, or help people; it's in my very nature to want to help, and I do so as often as I can, whenever someone is willing to listen. Over the years I think my own kids would say I preached about money and finance more than anything else. I'm sure my friends and family members even get tired of hearing it at times. I feel a responsibility somehow, to share and pass on what I've learned during my life.

Back in 1984, I was totally frustrated with my personal finances. I was always broke before it was even close to payday, even though I made a fair wage. It was at that time that I took an interest in getting educated on finance and money matters. I don't have a college education, and I don't really want to go out and get one at this stage in my life, and that's okay for me. However, I was able to seek out good financial advice and increase my education with a little hard work, time, and effort on my part.

During the span of my career, understanding the industry I worked in came like second nature for me. My employer's management team recognized this quickly and routinely had me teaching others throughout my years of employment. I trained or educated others in all that I had learned from my humble beginnings with the company, while also performing my everyday responsibilities.

I have trained people on the job for over thirty years, and I believe it's the same as teaching. Some people understood what I was teaching, and some people didn't. It's no different for teachers in our schools. Some children learn from one way of teaching, and others need a different approach.

The one big difference I may have incorporated in

training myself is that I became aware I'd have to change with the times. When the current industry I worked in made changes, I adjusted with them. For example, things needed to be taught differently when the electric power industry was deregulated. It was no longer business as usual; I accepted the fact that things were changing and adapted accordingly. Today, our schools need a different approach; they also need to adapt to change! Since, in my opinion, times have indeed changed, the education system needs to change by adding new programs, such as finance and technology, and to get rid of any outdated subjects. I think subjects like this need to be look at more closely, in order for American children to compete with the rest of the world.

I don't pretend to know all of the changes our education system needs, but with your help, America, I know we can come up with several *great ideas*. Here are some of mine.

As mentioned earlier, we should teach these kids about finances and how to manage money. Students need to know why it's a good thing to save for the things they want and not just buy them without any real thought. They need to know how to invest for the future and also for the unknown expenses that will inevitably come up in life. They need to know why it's necessary to learn the difference between good debt and bad debt and just what that truly means.

Our children need a firm understanding of why it is necessary to have various types of insurance and what insurance can do for them. I'll discuss this issue a little later on, but by now, you get my meaning. In addition, I believe that we fail to teach accountability, good health techniques, proper diet, and nutrition to young American students in a way that appeals to them. Let's take more time to educate them on those subjects. A healthy lifestyle promotes good brain activity and will hopefully help American kids learn better and, therefore, want to achieve more. A healthy body just makes you feel better about yourself and gives you the energy needed to face the day. I think social media has a responsibility to its young viewers to portray a healthy, happy, and responsible young adult as being more desirable than a fashionable young adult or one with the latest phone. What a joke to envy another because socially it's more acceptable to have the latest gadget than to have a brain.

Students need to be more aware of social development, which includes topics such as the dangers of poor hygiene, using protection during sex, and sexually transmitted diseases. I know this is old news and been taught for years—but the education has had little effect. We need to somehow teach these kids to be responsible about such things. Here in America, young kids having babies out of wedlock, once considered taboo, has now become socially acceptable. My educated guess is this seemingly accepted trend costs the taxpayers thousands of dollars every year, all due to the fact that these young teenagers are not held accountable for their actions. We have all heard about high school "clubs" of young high school girls actually trying to get pregnant, as if this is a desirable attribute; one Eastern high school reported seventeen girls pregnant. What was the purpose?

These young people need to be taught and held accountable for their choices and actions. Lord knows their parents aren't getting the point across. All these kids see is how easy it is to get out of any real commitments. That's why it's become so widely accepted to divorce at the first signs of trouble. If kids were taught family planning, respect for others, and love, imagine what might happen.

I think we should teach students to work together in groups as well as independently. In the real world, groups of individuals or committees of men and women typically solve problems. So why not use that to their advantage and teach it to American students at a young age?

This idea that you must do all of your studying and testing on your own may not be the best way to educate anymore, in my opinion. Our kids definitely need to learn to read, write, and spell, and learn history and math, as taught in the past and present, but when was the last time you did math without the aid of modern technology? When was the last time you went into an office and noticed the employees writing out their work by hand?

Obviously not since the technology boom—they use computers in the workplace. So why not educate students by focusing more on all of the advantages that the computer has to offer? Let's make that a main priority in their young lives.

Ever see a kid with a Game Boy or a cell phone? They can run circles around most adults with these things. I have seen young kids use a cell phone to do things I had no idea a cell phone was capable of doing. Our kids are able to beat the computer games they play in no time. These students can text message at the speed of sound. So, if all this is true, just imagine what might happen if they were taught in school using these same principles and tools. Imagine a program that would depict any given scenario of their choosing, such as a fourteen-year-old having a baby and what realistically they could expect as a consequence of that choice. That is a program with limitless possibilities that we could use to really educate with and get the real results from.

The youth in America are not dumb or unable to be educated properly. It's just that some of the methods we use to teach them are outdated and need to be updated, to say the least. Let's tap into all of the resources available today and make educating American students exciting and fun at the same time. Kids will love that. They should also learn at a much faster rate, and America, we all stand to gain from that!

Let me share a personal experience. In 1986, the power plant I worked in was once again making changes. My employer decided to cross-train its managing supervisors and new engineers together. Until that time, most first-line management employees were educated in only one side of the business—turbines, boilers, or the electrical side of the power plant operations. Now we were all going to cross-train in each area to make us more informed and well-rounded supervisors in all areas of operations. (By the way, this would ultimately eliminate the need for three managers on shift and drop it to just one, saving the company money.) By this time, I had been at the plant for ten years. I had already taken the initiative to learn the other areas of the plant operations, even though my background was in the electrical operating side. I was placed into a six-month training program with five other men, all of them engineers. Some were mechanical engineers and others electrical, all fresh out of college and newly hired. As our instructor taught us, it was just like any other school I had attended and just as in grade school, we were given tests and were required to pass them all. If not, there was a real possibility of losing your job. (Not unionized anymore, the company could do as it liked, pretty much.)

Anyway, as the six of us took each test, it became apparent that I had a firm understanding of all three operations already. One engineer in particular (a very sharp man by all accounts) would consistently ask me questions when he became confused. Naturally, I helped him understand how things worked, and along the way, we became good pals. He depended on me quite a bit.

Once our instructor would hand out the tests we were required to take, he would almost always leave the room and come back later. While the instructor was gone, my pal the young engineer, along with some of the other engineers, would ask me for help with the answers to the questions, and, right or wrong, I helped them. When the instructor came back, he would just gather up the tests like any other teacher would have done back when I was in grade school. Later on, we would receive our tests back after they were graded.

All five of the engineers would somehow ace the tests, and my tests always had some small part of the answers to the questions wrong—at least, according to the instructor. I received good grades but never as high as the others.

I asked this engineer whom I had become friends with, what he thought I was doing wrong. He told me that, while in college, he had learned to just write down as much as he could when answering the essay-style questions. That way, even if he was dead wrong, maybe something he put down might get him some credit for his response to the question. So I tried to elaborate as much as I could to see if that would work. But it didn't.

Frustrated, I asked all five men to copy my answers to the test we were taking word for word. They all agreed to do just that. When the graded test came back, it was the same old story; my grade was just a little lower than everyone else's. I called the instructor out on it right away in front of all the others.

"What's wrong with my answers? Didn't you notice we all had word-for-word responses? We all cheated," I said. The instructor did not seem fazed in the least. His only response to me was this: "Your grades are lower because all the engineers have a college education, and you don't." He added, "And that's the end of the story!" Then, with a smirk on his face, he turned away and went about his business, and nothing more was said about it.

Now, I would say that this was a classic example of that instructor's not being able to accept change (not to mention being a bit prejudiced in his thinking). I also think this illustrates two things: First, he believed, without a doubt, that a person with a college education needed to be treated differently, for some reason. Second, it shows there is a lot to be said for on-the-job training as well as an education attained from good schooling.

A college degree is a very good idea, and I strongly recommend it, but it's not the only way to go. When did corporate America decide that a worker with experience on the job did not equate to an educated employee? We need to keep an open mind and make wise, educated decisions from now on and not ignore a cry for change in the school system as we know it. So, once more I ask: *Why not open your eyes, Old World thinkers, and start doing what is best for all?*

Let's do what's best for American kids who may never be able to afford a college education. Instead of accepting the "the old ways are the best ways" mentality we've grown so comfortable with, let's educate students at the youngest possible age and put our tax dollars to the betterment of all. Let's get the United States back on track and strengthen the minds of our children and Americas future!

Energy

Moving on, I would now like to tackle the energy crisis issues we face in this country today. Americans all know that oil prices have been on a wild ride now for some time. Until just the last few weeks of September and October in 2008, prices had steadily climbed to an average of $4 a gallon at the pumps. With the majority of the population in this country already fighting to make ends meet, the high fuel costs made a bad economic situation even worse. The ripple effect of high-priced fuel has affected the cost of more than just America's personal transportation costs. Even though we witnessed a drop in gas prices, consumers continue to pay the higher costs of all products affected by this increase.

The cost of diesel fuel has reached an even higher level and has sustained the higher cost for a much longer time now than regular, unleaded gasoline. That was not the case in years past. Everything consumable and nonconsumable that is shipped in, out, and across this country requires the use of fuel one way or another. With the fuel costs escalating, so does the cost of moving product. That, in turn, raises prices on practically everything we Americans use in our daily lives. Companies are forced to pass these additional fuel and shipping costs on to the consumer. They do this so they can continue to show profits to shareholders and investors, as well as to keep their employees working. It becomes a vicious circle.

America's dependency on oil needs to be addressed right now, and it will take more than just talk. For years now, the news media has provided scores of reports that burning oil is a major factor when it comes to environmental pollution. Cleaning up the air quality should be motivation enough for people everywhere to take action; after all, it's what keeps us alive and healthy, not to mention what influences our children's health in the future.

Oil and oil byproducts are used in so many different applications; however, it will be next to impossible to eliminate the use of oil totally. So let's look at some things we as Americans already know. According to reports from the Energy Information Administration and from Web sites like naturalgas.org, in America natural gas reserves are more abundant than oil. We also know that automobiles can and, in some cases, have been converted to natural gas use. It only makes sense to me to immediately take a closer look at this alternative.

Converting our cars and trucks to natural gas now will buy the American people some time, giving scientists and engineers the opportunity to develop new forms of energy alternatives, such as hydrogen-powered and electric-powered automobiles. This alternative would most definitely reduce some of America's dependency on oil. Again, according to data from the Energy Information Administration, burning natural gas as opposed to oil will also cut down on pollution. I think that should help stabilize or even lower fuel costs in the long run. This sounds like a win-win situation for the American people and the world's environment. If this action is taken, then fueling stations across America will have to install natural gas pumps for the public to use. Americans will need to be educated on the proper usage of both this new fuel source and its equipment and so on. I realize there's a lot more that needs to be done than that, but it's definitely doable. I encourage the people and experts aware of this alternative to step up and take the bull by the horn.

I think America can also use some help understanding how alternative sources of electrical power generation can help us all. This is the industry where I have worked most of my life, so I speak with firsthand, or hands-on experience. Today, some of the most widely used resources for generating electricity are oil, natural gas, coal, nuclear, hydro, and pump storage facilities. You may have also heard about solar, wind, and geothermal sources of electric power. These types of electric generators are not as widely used, due to Mother Nature's control over them. They can be and are being used today—quite cost-effectively, I might add—but they aren't as reliable as the other more commonly used types of generation.

If we Americans want to reduce the amount of oil, coal, and natural gas used to make electricity, there are numerous hurdles to overcome. The biggest hurdle, in my opinion, will be that all electrical power producers have to work together. Let me say that again: *all of them have to be on board!*

Let me explain why. It is true that we can add more cost-efficient power like nuclear, wind, and so on, to reduce both oil dependency and reduce pollution, and that's the good news. I even have more good news, but you will need to know how the power grid works to truly understand. This is a very crude explanation by industry standards, and I admit it might be somewhat confusing. Here goes. In America today, now that the utilities have been deregulated, there are even more moving parts to the electric power equation than ever before. There are companies that produce power, also known as the generators of electricity. There are the transmission providers, also known as the lines that carry the electricity from the power generators to our homes and businesses. There are power marketers; these are businesses that own some of the power generated by the power producers, and they also own transmission rights in various parts of the country. Confused yet?

When electricity is made, it must be used immediately. It can't be stored, like natural gas or oil, in the ground or in barrels. It is generated and consumed by industry and by people like you and me, right then and there in our homes and businesses. This generated power is also traded like any other commodity. Electricity is sold to and from power marketing firms and utilities all across the United States, ultimately to supply their customers.

At home you get billed monthly for your electric consumption by what is known as your power provider. These power providers have choices. They can either make their own electricity or they can buy it on the open market. These same power providers also have to purchase the transmission rights to get that generated electric power to their customers. These transactions are done each and every hour of every day of the year. There is no stopping them, or the lights go out.

In today's electric marketplace, the price of generated power and transmission changes with the available supply and customer demand, and not so much by the cost to make the electricity. It is the trader's job to get the most money they can for this power and transmission. Some of the electrical providers' biggest limiting factors are outages; more simply put, the equipment is not available at the power plants or on the transmission lines, for one reason or another, along with power flow and voltage control issues, both of which are essential to the delivery of usable electricity, but it's not important that you understand this part. Just know the above-mentioned information is important to utility companies everywhere.

Imagine your car is the power plant. You need fuel to make the power that is necessary to move your vehicle. Now imagine the roads we travel on as the transmission system. Without the roads, you can't go anywhere. Simple enough, right? Now let's add some variables.

Each car costs a different amount to purchase, just like the different types of power plants cost different amounts to build, depending on their type. Some cars run further on a gallon of gas, just like some power plants can produce lower-cost, more efficient energy, depending on the type of fuel used. Your car breaks down from time to time, so you need to get repairs done. You also need a backup of some sort when this happens. You get a ride from some other source. Perhaps a friend drives you, or you take the bus, and so forth.

Power plants, likewise, break down from time to time or need maintenance; they also need backup sources of generation. So, there are power plants on standby or plants that are not run at full capacity all of the time.

At different times of the year, gas prices go up and down, depending on demand. In America, we almost always see prices at the pumps go up around holidays and in the summertime when people tend to drive more. The same thing happens every day to electricity. At night, when demand for electric power is low, prices come down, and during the peak hours, typically during the morning and evening hours, electric load demand is up, and so are the prices.

If you're driving down a road, and it is flat, your car runs with very little effort, and it is cost-effective. Once you come to a hill, though, you need to add more gas to climb that hill and vice versa when you go down the hill. Power providers need to do the same thing with electricity. As most of us sleep at night, power consumption is flat for the most part. When we wake and start the day, power consumption goes up and down as we use electric devices, just like the car on the hills in my example.

Transmission is a little easier to understand. If we assume transmission lines are the streets and roads we use to get around, then people have to realize they are all toll roads, but with one exception—the toll changes at every turn. That is because transmission providers can change the amount they charge as they see fit. Supply and demand!

Okay, now you have a little background on how the electrical system works, but this next part gets a little more complex.

In order to cut back on the pollution from using oil and coal and to also reduce American dependency on oil, we need alternatives. America, I believe we can add more nuclear power plants or wind power systems to the power grid (also known as the transmission system); that should be no problem. Some major transmission owners may have to beef up the transmission system in their areas to handle the new generation, of course, and that's going to cost someone. Even more important than that, who's going to build those power plants America needs to free itself from coal, oil, and their pollution, and where will the demand for those plants be located?

There are basically three electrical transmission grids or systems in the United States. The first includes all of the states east of the Rocky Mountains, from Canada to the southern coast. This is considered one grid or system, with all states tied together by transmission lines. Just a side note—the United States is also tied to the Canadian transmission system. Second, there is the system west of the Rocky Mountains from Canada to Mexico. Lastly, there is Texas, which is a system unto itself.

Today, the way electrical systems work, utilities *have* to make room for any increase in generation on their transmission system. Remember, however, they can't store it. So, if these power providers don't have a demand for the extra power, then it runs over from one provider's system where it was generated into some other provider's system. Keep in mind that almost all systems are connected from state to state across the country. This additional generation can cause all kinds of problems. It can overload transmission lines, causing them to trip out (shut down), thus interrupting the flow of power into our homes and businesses.

Then there is the cascading effect to worry about. When one transmission line goes down, power must find another path to flow into. When that happens, there is the real possibility that the change in power flow will overload other transmission lines or even the power plants themselves. You've all heard of this—it's called a blackout. Not so long ago, in August 2003, Michigan, Ohio, New Jersey, New York, and other parts of the Northeast (eight states in total were affected, in addition to parts of Canada) experienced a blackout.

So, as you can see, there are a lot of moving parts to this electrical system, and I have not even touched on them all. Now that I've provided a generic synopsis of the power and usage of electricity, let's get back to the big problem, which is how we can reduce our oil use and pollution. All of these companies (power producers and providers) have to get together and plan to expand the grid as a whole. Trying to get them all to work together is a big challenge; never forget that greed and profits will play a vital role. If power generators do add more nuclear power plants to an area, the problem of minimum load will become an issue as well. Also, overloading of the transmission lines could become a problem.

To define minimum load, let's assume that we the customers consume only 50 percent of the power made from the power generators that are running during the off-peak hours (at night, typically). Then during the day, we consume 95 percent of the power made from those same power plants (we keep some in reserve in case of loss of generation or higher load demands than predicted). Those power plants that are kept running at all times, will need to be ramped up and ramped back down several times during a twenty-four hour period (as demand goes up and down). If the plants in this example can't back down far enough to get to the 50 percent load demand level, it spills over into the neighboring system (which provides free power for that system). Of course, power providers are not in business to give it away free.

Nuclear power does not regulate very well (move up and down), so it then becomes what the industry calls base load power. As people and industry go through their regular daily routines, power providers need units that can regulate. Power demands change constantly when we turn electrical equipment on and off, both at home and at the workplace. Coal, natural gas, and oil provide power companies with the ability to follow these minute-to-minute power consumption changes. This is due to the fact that they can move up and down very quickly, whereas nuclear power generators or wind power generators cannot.

If the power provider's base load exceeds 50 percent but not the 95 percent (which I am still using for this example) with the nuclear plants running, they then need to back down the more costly power like oil, gas, and coal. This happens every day all across the land, and it's a good thing for more reasons than I need to explain just now.

Consequently, when you back down all the power

plants that are on line and running, and these power plants still can't get down below minimum load demand, it leaves power producers with only a few options. One, they can sell their excess power if there is a market for it. Two, they can take the higher cost units off line all together, but that's not a good idea in most cases. Or three, they can give the power away free (since there is no way to store it).

One more thing I would like to share with you is the push we are seeing to use wind and solar power as ways to reduce our dependency on oil. Both good ideas ... but power providers need to make what they call in the industry, a load forecast. Simply put, that is an educated guess regarding how much electricity they will need for every minute of every day to meet their customers' demands. Once they make that forecast, they then need to be certain they have enough power generation to meet the forecasted load demand. They do that by using all of the available sources of generation they have at their disposal. Or they can go out and purchase the power from a provider that has an excess. Purchasing power is actually sometime more cost-effective for the providers.

The lack of dependability of wind and solar power makes it *almost* impossible to count on. Power providers need to meet their forecast (or demand) and also have adequate reserves, in case of unforeseen troubles.

Taking all of these factors into account, being cost-effective with resources means using wind, solar, and nuclear, but gas and oil units will always be needed for reserves. That's because those types of generation can be brought on line (turned on) in less than thirty minutes; in most cases, fifteen minutes is the requirement. Nuclear and coal-fired power plants take several hours and sometime days to bring on line. That takes too long when electricity demand is required right now by everyone. Americans are accustomed to being able to turn it on and receive it right then.

There is yet another type of power generation that I feel will solve a lot of our problems here in America. It provides a clean source of generation and will help with *most* of the minimum load issues caused by the addition of nuclear power plants or wind generators, should this country chose to go that way. It is, however, used only in a very limited amount today. You can ask anyone who works to meet a power provider's load demand, and they'll tell you they wish they had a lot more of it. It's a wonderful resource to have at your disposal.

So what is it? It's called a pump storage facility. A pump storage system, simply put, works like this: Water is held in a reservoir or lake, high above on a hill, and below is another reservoir. In between, you have water driven turbines. Those in turn drive electricity-producing generators. These same generators can be reversed to become motors and run pumps. Water flows by gravity down large water tubes, driving the turbines and the generators, thus producing electricity.

This water is collected in the lower reservoir. Then, typically at night, the flow of water is changed, and the generators become motors used to run a pump. The "motor" now pumps that same water back up into the upper reservoir. Now, it is ready for use once again.

Simple enough and very clean. The drawback is that it takes more electricity than these generators produce to pump the water back uphill. It's roughly a one-third loss of power as any current owners of such facilities can tell you, *or refer to the Internet, at sites like Wikipedia.org for more detailed explanation.* In other words, if it takes three megawatts of power to pump water up into the reservoir, you only get two megawatts back out when you drain the reservoir. A megawatt is equal to one million watts.

That is not necessarily a bad thing, especially if power producers add more nuclear power plants. As I discussed earlier, nuclear power should be base loaded and not moved up and down. Nuclear power is one of the most cost-effective (cheapest) sources of generating electrical power. So why not use excess nuclear power to pump back up the reservoirs at those pump storage facilities at night? The less expensive cost of nuclear power will more than offset the losses or difference between pumping and generating at the pump storage facilities. That should make the utility businesses happy with a strong bottom line. If power-generating companies build more nuclear power and more pump storage facilities, it will allow America to significantly reduce the amount of coal, oil, and natural gas used, and that can only be good for everyone. So far, for me at least, I can find no one who will listen. I have tried to contact politicians both in the House and Senate, businessmen, billionaires, the news media, and utility CEOs, and I have received no response, but I will not give up.

It will take a lot of work to get everyone on board and working for the greater good when it comes to the current energy crisis. I've given some ideas on how to go about it, so if this country can put aside greed for the benefit of all, maybe my suggestions could work.

One last thing for those who are worried about

nuclear waste: how hard can it be to put it back in the ground safely? Come on, government. Cut through the red tape, and make it happen! Americans, with all our ingenuity, skills, and knowledge, can surely collectively figure out this dilemma.

Rambling

The question of Social Security has been a topic of discussion as long as I can remember. The Social Security Act was drafted by President Roosevelt's committee on economic security. The act was an attempt to limit what were seen as dangers in the modern American life, including old age, poverty, unemployment, and the burdens of widows and fatherless children. By passing this act, President Roosevelt became the first president to advocate the protection of the elderly. President Roosevelt signed the Social Security Act on August 14, 1935. For more details, visit the government Web site http://www. ssa.gov/.

For years, people have heard that the Social Security program will run out of money. But the truly salient question, which no one seems to be able to answer, is *when?* We all wonder if there will be enough left when we get to that magic age. People who receive the benefits now ask, *Will I continue to receive that money?*

Most of us have paid into the Social Security program for as long as we've been employed, along with our employers on our behalf. Now we are told, *guess what? The system is broke; it's not working the way it was intended to work.*

Many Americans are depending on Social Security to fund their retirements. Now what will they do? All the money Americans thought they were saving is gone. You're now working for more than just yourself; you work for everyone receiving Social Security currently, as well as in the future, until the system runs out. Does that sound fair to you?

As I recall, President Bush told America he was going to work hard for us and fix the system. Of course, this was something he was never able to accomplish. Oh, all the politicians agree that something must be done, but, as usual, they can't agree on what. With each new idea that was presented in Congress, these men and women who represent the American people could not seem to get what they wanted out of it.

I heard one solution floating around that included allowing people to invest part of the money they now put into the Social Security program for themselves. But it was shot down. Politicians basically said they couldn't let us do our own investing, not of even part of the Social Security monies, because we are not qualified in such matters. Besides, the government had to be thinking about where the shortfall, hence created due to no longer receiving full Social Security payments, would come from. Bad idea everyone, so let's just not do anything, okay?

I guess it was okay to change other tax acts such as in 1974, when the 401(k) and other such retirement savings programs were introduced. They call it the Employee Retirement Income Security Act (ERISA). In case you did not realize, these retirement programs are *tax laws*. (You can learn more about ERISA at http://www.dol. gov/ebsa/compliance_assistance.html.)

Don't you have to ask yourself why those tax laws were put into effect in the first place? I think it was so that employers and politicians could gain something—but what, I wonder? Things of that nature don't just happen out of the blue. There is always something lurking in the shadows. Just like Social Security reform. Why haven't the powers that be in Washington fixed it yet? Maybe it's just too hard, so they choose to do nothing and hope the problem will just go away.

So what did Washington and employers gain when they let employees invest for their retirements instead of relying on the traditional employer (defined benefit) pension plans that most big companies carried for their employees? Remember, the American people were also counting on the backup of Social Security.

Well, one thing politicians knew back then was that the Social Security system was going to fail, so my guess is Washington needed to do something to get the American people saving for retirement, to avoid the big headaches later! Another thing happened when ERISA was passed. The burden of retirement savings was passed on to the employees and off of the employers. Employers no longer had to put money away for their employee's retirement, and that was a huge burden lifted off them. No longer were the large retirement funds needed for the big business owners.

Employers only had to offer a 401(k) or one of the other types of savings plans to employees. Now, even though employers do not have to, some do match part of the money people invest. That makes employees feel like their employers are still doing some good for them, and they are, just not as much as some employers once did.

All this saved money is, in turn, tax-deferred until the employee reaches age fifty-nine-and-a-half, at which time they can, if they chose to, start withdrawing from the savings, or seventy-and-a-half, at which time he or she must start withdrawing it. Those two things sounded great to employees, but were they really? Now, instead of the burden being on the employer to guarantee retirement payments until retirees passed away, it became the employee's burden. As most of you know, you're not savvy investors or even good savers.

I mention this because now people had to become familiar with the stock market, bond market, and mutual funds. Most of us had never even take any interest in such things. I guess, back then, Washington felt this was an okay move. A way to help with the problems the Social Security system was going to have in the future. But our government won't trust Americans, not today with even part of their Social Security money. Do I have the answer to the Social Security problem? No, but once again I have some food for thought.

If Washington is going to bail out the financial markets in America to the tune of who knows how many billions, a bailout for crooks, in my opinion, then maybe our government should take the money and fix the Social Security system instead. At least take a portion of the interest they receive back and put it toward the shortfall in the Social Security system. As long as the American government will be carrying people's home loans anyway, why not set aside 1 percent of the interest repayment from the billions of dollars lent out? Take the money after repayment is made, and use it for the good of all in America. At the same time, Washington can still pay back whoever gave them the money in the first place.

Here's an idea. Let's stop taking Social Security from American workers born after 1990 going forward. Let's allow them an option to take that same Social Security money and put it into safe investments of the employee's choice. There are still safe places to invest today. All government needs to do is allow employers to make those investments available as an investment plan for employees, just like the 401(k) programs. If it were up to me, I would do this as a requirement, just as the government takes money out now as Social Security. This will then give the government a clear number of the *bailout* dollars required to meet the needs of the Social Security program as it exists now. You want stimulus? That should stimulate people!

Remember earlier, when I spoke about ERISA and what's in it for the government? Well, all of that tax-deferred money that American employees invested will be taxed at age seventy-and-a-half, when withdrawn, right? So, if the government stands to gain all this new tax money, why not use it to cover the shortfall in the Social Security system? Now if you couple that with the change I proposed earlier, allowing people born after 1990 the choice of safe investments for their retirement, and you have a plan. It would be a start anyway.

Too bad the one thing Washington did not count on was the deep drop in the stock market we've experienced recently. Most Americans have had their life savings and 401(k) cut by half at a time when the government was expecting to receive a fresh supply of tax dollars from retiring baby boomers. Looks like our government will have to get the revenue some other way! I'm sure there are solutions to these problems. In the meantime, there will be a lot of discontented American people until those solutions are found or until the government hears people like me and takes action.

More Rambling, Does Crime Really Pay in America, Still?

Our government has so much "fat" in it that I'm certain we can cut way back somewhere. How about we cut back on the spending in our prison systems? Not that the employees need a cutback, but let's cut back on the spending for inmates. We can possibly kill two birds with one stone.

The way I see it, we would divert money back to the taxpayers who worked hard for it, if we cut the prisoners off. We can possibly help drop the crime rate at the same time.

Here's how it might work. We don't let prisoners interact with each other at all. We feed them the same food every day of their sentence. No more TV. No more visits. No more phone calls. The men can all wear pink jumpsuits, and the women can wear lime green for all I care. If we cut back on all the little extra things inmates get, who's going to want to commit a crime again and risk going back to jail?

We spend an inordinate amount of money keeping these criminals in their own little worlds, and they come out worse, in many instances. Imagine how it would be to sit in the same cell day after day with no recreation, no conversations, and the same food for every meal. Give them hell, just as they did to whomever, when they committed their crimes. Too hard on them, you say? Tough! Save all of us taxpayers the money, and put that money to some good!

Some of the men and women in jail today don't really need to be treated so harshly. We should try to educate them, but at their own expense. These institutions can and should figure out ways that inmates can work for their schooling and reform. You know there's an old saying that if you have to pay for it, you're going to appreciate it more. It's only fair to offer a better life to those who really want it.

With a proper education, inmates can re-enter into society and become good, productive citizens. I think some of the younger inmates just need to be pointed in the right direction. But if we keep the first time or soft-core type criminals in with the hardcore criminals, that's what they will become themselves. Who knows what could happen with the proper motivation? I'm rambling on here, still hoping that Americans can see an area where they might step up and do some real good rather than sit back doing nothing, as in the past. The American people need to demand cutbacks in our government spending on ineffective programs where the taxpaying citizens suffer as much if not more than unreformed or unrepentant criminals.

How about the illegal immigrants who cross our borders each and every day? Our government spends a ton of tax dollars on trying to stop these people from coming across the border and also on catching them once they are in the United States. Maybe we need a different approach? Let's offer them jobs repairing our roads and bridges or building some of those power systems changes we need. Tell them, *As long as you come to America, you must work first and also learn our language.* If illegal immigrants in this country want to become citizens here, they need to adhere to our laws. We don't really have to compensate them too much—just enough for some food and shelter is all, like any other American who works for a living. Illegal immigrants are here working cheaply as it is anyway, so let's take full advantage of the situation. The government can then tax all these once-illegal people and put that money to good use, once they gain citizenship and employment. But both citizenship and employment must be viewed as prerequisites, along with learning to speak English!

Our government putting money to good use is a far-fetched idea, but who knows, it could happen. I'm not really all that bad, folks. I just want something done, so I'm trying to get your creative side thinking. If politicians would just find a way to work together for the greater good of all, I'm sure they could come up with ideas that would save America. Let's get out of the mess we're in. Right now! Not ten years from now!

And Still More Ramblings:
I'm Taxed Out

Taxes make up the largest accounted for and unaccounted for expenses in the average American budget today. Can we be taxed any more than we already are? If the politicians have their way, you bet we can. How else can they fund all of the items on their agendas? Don't we all as Americans get just a little tired of working and seeing our paychecks go everywhere but into our own pockets?

We work and pay taxes, we buy food and pay taxes, and we drive our cars and trucks and pay taxes, in addition to paying taxes on the fuel used to operate them. What it comes down to is just this: we can't do anything and not pay taxes. From the moment we are born, we are taxed in one way or another. Every item we buy has been taxed over and over again before we even purchase it and pay tax once again. We are even taxed on our tax refunds! Get that straight in your head. Let's say you pay in more tax than you needed to pay. It is then refunded to you after you file a tax return. It then becomes taxable income once more the next year. Keep in mind that you will pay tax on that same money year after year with every refund you receive. Sound good to you? I didn't think so. Where is all this tax money going?

Liquor is taxed, cigarettes are taxed, and gasoline is taxed, and so on before we purchase them. Federal, state, and local governments add taxes on top of taxes to fund what? I'll bet that money is spent primarily for helping people like you and me, right? I'm sure that if we look at taxes from a different perspective, we can find ways that even the air we breathe has been taxed. No free air—sorry, folks! None that's clean anyway. You can't give me one example of anyone living in this country today that has not been adversely affected by taxes.

Now, some politicians would have us believe we need increased taxes to keep things like our roads and bridges in repair. But did we or did we not pay for those same repairs when we paid our federal and state taxes in the first place? Also, why do local governments in turn add even more taxes (added sales taxes and property taxes) on to the things we own and purchase? So they can make repairs to the roads? Or wait—what about the tolls we pay on many of the roads we travel? Remember our politicians' promises about the tolls? They said they were going to improve the road system for us, the American people, so they needed to add a *temporary* toll. Toll, tax same thing!

It was only going to be imposed until the new road or repairs were paid for, so politicians said! On how many toll roads have you seen the tolls lowered or taken away? I bet the answer is none. I know I haven't seen that happen as promised. As a matter of fact, if you now use those same toll roads and don't have a pass, you're charged even more. Paying cash gets you punished. Motorists from out of state or those who seldom use the tollways locally slow down the traffic that the tollbooth created in the first place, so they must pay more!

On a recent trip to Illinois, I was shocked to see that in five years the tolls had doubled from my last trip using the toll system there. If you were to sit and just watch the number of cars and trucks that go through at just one of these tollbooths for an hour, and then figure the income from that tollbooth, you would be astonished. Give any of us that money, and we would be rich in no time.

There are tollbooths every few miles around Chicago, and tens of thousands of cars pass through them every day. A cheap toll is fifty cents, but most are $1.00 to $1.50, and to get from point A to point B, people must pass through at least two tollbooths. One toll when they get on and then another when they get off.

I drove from Aurora, Illinois, to Joliet, Illinois, using the tollway system not long ago. I paid sixty cents to get on, then the next toll was $1.00, and then I paid another $1.60 to get off. That's a total of $3.20 for a one-way trip. It took me about an hour to make that trip due to traffic. If I were to make that same trip every day back and forth, to and from work, for example, it would cost me $6.40 in tolls/taxes per day. Multiply that by five days a week, and that is $32.00 weekly. Heaven forbid, I need to go anywhere else.

Furthermore, this trip I mention cost me ten hours of my life in the car. Had I not used the toll road, it would have taken me twice as long for the same trip, if I was lucky! Don't we, as citizens, have enough bills to pay without all of the tolls and taxes we are charged in our lives daily? Again, I wish our government could show us where all that money is really going? I, for one, would like to know.

Oh, hey! How about the lotteries all across the land? Weren't they going to use part of that income to help make road repairs, not to mention fund American schools? This revenue stream should have cut taxes at least at state levels. What about the casinos that have popped up everywhere? Some of the funds from casinos were also going to help fix the roads and supplement the school systems. These institutions take in millions every week, but I've not seen my school or road taxes go down even a penny yet!

Could it be mismanagement in our governing systems and the greed of those people in charge of these programs that are to blame? Go ahead and take exception if you are one of the people working for these corrupt systems. But if you do, then please tell us all what you have done to fix these problems America faces, so we can give you the credit you have coming.

People in politics and managers of company's affairs are so worried that if they don't spend every dime they have been given for their budgets and agendas during the current year they receive the budget money that they won't get the same funding the next year. So they waste it on crap just to ensure spending it all, instead of using it for good, like truly helping the people of this country.

Taxes and big business! You must know that these two things go hand in hand! Big business gets so many different write-offs from the tax code as it exists that many don't even end up paying any income taxes at all. Tell me, when was the last time you paid no income taxes at all?

I'm not making this up. In fact, this is what big business strives for—not paying any taxes at all! These powerful businesses pay people to look for the loopholes in the tax code to get them out of paying. It's no wonder they are given more write-offs than an average worker is given. We, the working class, get the short end on taxes every time, not just some of the time.

The tax laws in this country are a joke, and big business and politicians are laughing in our faces over it. Our failure to do something about it is their dream come true. Every person who has ever run for public office has said he or she is going to do something about this tax problem. Yet public officials have failed to fix the problem for as long as any of us can remember!

In 2008, again we were hearing it from the two candidates running for president. One would cut taxes if elected, for the people who make so much money or less a year. The other would cut taxes for big business to help bring back jobs to America that have gone overseas. One would use a scalpel, the other a hatchet. But, mark my words, neither will help us. Not until the tax laws are totally revised so that taxes become fair for all, will any of us see our taxes cut. Here's an idea to lower taxes: eliminate the multitude of ridiculous programs that get funding from our hard-earned tax dollars. That would be a start. What if the American people could see in black and white what all their tax dollars are used for; would that blow your mind? Then we could offer advice on which government programs are really worthwhile or not and get them amended.

Here's another thought: simplify, so that Americans would all be able to understand, the tax codes. If you or I could understand the tax codes, we would not need help from the accountants and income tax firms that are on every corner. Think of the savings you'd get right there. After all, most of us only make peanuts, compared to businesses and politicians who should be the only ones needing these services.

Americans should be capable of doing their own taxes if they choose. Today, however, if you do choose to do your taxes, let's say using one of the computer software programs available, you need to keep in mind that that program may not be as easy as you might think or as advertised. That is due to the way current tax laws read. They are much too complicated to decipher and are constantly changing. You may be missing write-offs, or you may not be finding all the loopholes like businesses do. Besides all that, you will also be taxed on the purchase of the tax program.

Here's another thought: imagine if all of the money spent on campaigning on empty promises or mudslinging *were spent on truth?* One politician in 2008 had a television show running twenty-four hours a day, telling us Americans what a great guy he is. I'm sure that the cost to run that ad month after month was not cheap. Now, I understand that these politicians have to get the word out about themselves, but why not limit it to just the truth, for once?

Let's say the only campaigning political candidates can do is about verifiable achievements. Then, take all the rest of their campaign contributions and put those dollars to some really good use like saving America from higher taxes or putting crooked politicians and businessmen behind bars? Limiting campaigning to fact and redirection of campaign funds to help the people I could really support! Of course, it seems that something as sensible as this could never happen, at least not in our lifetime. Or could it?

I ask each citizen of the United States to do something. Let's take action and get a grip on these crooks. Ask yourself what you can do, and then find some way to help. Your vote is a way to start helping but not if we keep electing the same old way. We as Americans need a government that discloses the truth about the men and women we elect to office. Truth is a word that is not real anymore; it is just a distorted word used to get your vote.

You as a voting citizen need to be able to really see the issues for yourself by *reading and examining* what a person has actually accomplished and not be influenced solely by what the news media wants you to know. Only then can you make a choice, an informed choice, about real changes that appeal to you. In addition, we need television, radio, and newspapers to report the truth without bias.

People, it's time we got some help with these types of issues. Start a movement; get a petition going, insisting on change in government. Let's get our voices heard and responded to. Enough empty promises! We need to demand tough action, and that won't be easy to come by. That is why Americans need to step up with ideas that will help and that we can all live with. Start by demanding the truth from our elected officials. Ask where each and every tax dollar is spent, and ask them to make it public for all Americans to see. If the government were made to do this, then I'm sure politicians would be just as surprised as the American people would be at the waste in their own programs. At the very least, this would enforce the need for real change rather than just a lot of talk about change.

I've heard a lot of talk these days about health care and insurance and the lack of funds or the outrageous cost of these programs. I'll be the first to admit that understanding any insurance program is a tricky subject to take on. I don't always understand it myself; once again there are too many moving parts. Americans have just too much on their plates when it comes to this subject; that is why I suggested earlier to educate our kids early in grade school on the subject

We have auto, home, mortgage, health, dental, personal property, life, and vision care, just to name a few types of insurance available today. In short, insurance is you betting that you're going to need it for one reason or another and insurance companies betting you won't need it. One of the big problems today is people in this country have become so obsessed with suing the other guy that insurance has become a necessity not a luxury.

All across America, greed has driven the price of peace of mind almost out of reach for most. If you crash your car, you had better have insurance. If you get sick, you had better have insurance. If someone is visiting you at your home and, for example, a rocking chair rolls over his or her foot, you had better have insurance. It's no wonder why our rates are so high.

It is mostly because of greed. People feel they are due compensation under any and all circumstances, so they sue you. They collect for the dumbest things, because lawyers tell them to. Turn on the television, and you will most assuredly see a law firm shilling for your business. "Sue!" is their cry. "I can get you money!"

Or what about hospitals that charge outrageous prices? Like $5 for an aspirin. It's true. I was charged $5 for one aspirin way back in 1985—or I should say my insurance provider was charged that. The list of people and big businesses that are to blame is longer than a line stretching from coast to coast.

My wife suffers from rheumatoid arthritis and needs to receive infusions monthly, along with the chemotherapy drugs she takes weekly. These drugs and other medical supplies cost $5,479 per month. As she and I researched this debilitating illness, we found out that some medications cost upward of $10,000 per dose. These treatments will not cure the arthritis but are intended to only stop or slow its spread. As I understand it, there are thousands stricken by this illness each year. If this is what we have to look forward to for the rest of her life, something must change, or we will go broke! Our insurance will only cover so much, and the rest is up to us. We currently pay over $900 a month for our medical coverage.

She is just one person with one disease; millions of men and women all across the land have ailments as costly as this one, and some have much worse. With the price of treatments being so high, it's no wonder medical insurance is so expensive. Who is making a killing on these drugs? Big pharmaceutical companies, that's who. They do their research and discover new drugs and, in turn, put a price on them so high that most can't afford them. I understand these companies need to recoup their investments, but when do the prices come down? When will everyone be able to afford help?

Some type of regulations must be put on pharmaceutical companies, on hospitals, on doctors, and on emergency care facilities. They must be held accountable or somehow they must justify the prices they are charging. The American people are footing the bill for this greed, and it shows up in the form of higher insurance premiums.

Deregulation, in almost every case, was intended to create competition and reduce costs to the public, but in almost every case, deregulation has only driven costs up even more. Remember when the natural gas, electrical, and phone companies were deregulated? Not one of those bills you received came down after deregulation; they all went up because of greed. It's no different in the insurance business or for the drug manufacturers. Without some means to an end, the sky's the limit when it comes to prices. Some type of intervention is needed if we are to get insurance under control.

(Recent changes have taken place in insurance lawsuits, as I understand it. Now, if there is a loss of limb or damage and loss of usage of a limb, some state laws cap a maximum reimbursement for that loss. If a person looses, say 20 percent usage of his or her arm, it now will equate to a maximum payout and no more. One of the problems I see in these types of circumstances is this may allow one person to continue to work with 20 percent loss and another not to be able to.)

If we could live without insurance, I know everyone would, but, alas, it's a way of life today, so we need to deal with it. Heck, nowadays, you can't even die without insurance coverage because the cost of a funeral is so high! Maybe we should push for legislation passing a law that requires insurance companies to provide one policy that covers all. Funny as that may seem, that would be one way to offset the cost of rising health insurance: one-stop coverage.

In a way, that is how insurance works anyway. You purchase, for example, auto coverage. If you never have an accident, you don't get a refund at the end of your driving life. All you did was bet that you would have an accident, and the insurance company wins, because you didn't. That's how insurance companies pay for the others who did have an accident—with your money. Maybe there should be some sort of required total-person-coverage insurance. It would cover you and all your possessions and actions during your life. Imagine how much money we could save on our premiums if all the good drivers' and healthy people's premiums helped defer the cost, like in our auto insurance, example.

I think we need some sort of actions to be taken in regards to pharmaceutical companies, hospitals, and doctors. Making money is one thing, but helping mankind is more important than greed! Also, we need to do something about all of the lawyers—or ambulance chasers, as I like to refer to them. The entire above-mentioned group, along with others, have a hand in the American people's lives through costly insurance premiums.

Once again, it is because of people like them that all of us honest people pay through the nose for insurance. Just watch television, and see all the ads for lawyers looking to capitalize on your so-called misfortune. Politicians, lawyers, big drug manufacturers, and the insurance companies should be held accountable to all of us for these atrocities!

Now, not all of the men and women in these industries are nefarious or greedy people; some really do care. I have had great doctors and health care providers who have taken care of me most of my life. It's like anything else: a few bad apples spoil the whole bunch. It is up to all of us as Americans to report those bad apples to the proper agencies if we are to see hope of reform. In my mind, it's like watching the news. Most of what we see is bad news because that's what sells or keeps people interested. But I am sure that good news stories would outweigh the bad if reported more often. Americans just need to demand action against the terrible things they see taking place and not just accept them.

Last year, I had an experience that just made me so upset. I was working around the house when the phone rang. It was my dentist's office calling. The woman on the other end of the line informed me that I needed to schedule an appointment before the end of the year. I told her that I had been in just a month or so earlier for my six-month checkup, and that everything had been fine. She then went on to say that if I did not come in, I would not have used up all my insurance coverage for the year. I said, "So you want me to come in just to use up my allotted coverage for the year?"

"Yes," she said, "or you will lose it!"

More like, *you won't squeeze all the money you can out of both me and my insurance provider!*

This is the type of thing that drives all our rates up; needless to say, I stopped using that dentist. I can't stomach that kind of behavior, and I wish more people would feel as I do.

Upon reflection, what I should have done is reported the dentist to my insurance company. I would then hope they could take action against such practices. I am happy to say that I have found a great dentist who shows genuine concern for my well-being and has very reasonable rates. You have to work a little at it, but you can and will find good professional help that cares and still puts you before greed.

Ever wonder why you see those ads on television saying, *Come to us, and we will compare auto insurance rates for you?* Then, the rates they give you are compared to three other major insurance providers, but their rate is always the lowest. If you want to do a little test of your own, try this one: Back in 1984, I received some good advice when it came to choosing an auto insurance provider. I was told to pick one of the major providers only. Then I was told to call several of their local agents for a quote. Now, at the time, this seemed a little strange; after all, the agents all represented the same insurance company. But I did it anyway—after I was assured I would be enlightened. Enlightened I was. Not one of the agents I called gave me the same quote, and the prices varied by several hundred dollars a year for the same coverage.

So I decided to do the test again here in 2008. The only difference this time is that I asked for quotes for auto coverage, life insurance, and home insurance. I chose a major provider that you have all heard of before: Allstate. It took me about four hours to gather this information, with all of it done over the phone. I made sure to ask for quotes using the exact same figures each time. I asked for auto insurance quotes on a 2007 model SUV using $100,000/$300,000 coverage with a $500/$500 deductible, $25,000/$50,000 uninsured motorist limits, and $100 roadside towing. The first number is the maximum dollars the insurance company will pay one person for an accident (in this case $100,000), and the second represents the maximum payout for all injured in the crash, regardless of the number of people involved. On the homeowner's insurance, I used $250,000 dwelling replacement cost coverage with 75 percent personal property coverage or roughly $190,000, $500,000 personal liability, and also used a $1,000 deductible. I asked for two different quotes for life insurance, for a $100,000 and a $150,000 policy on a male who was fifty years old, a nonsmoker in good health. Both quotes were for term policies that had a fixed price for the next fifteen years.

The following figures are the results of my little test done October 27, 2008.

	Auto	Home	Life
Agent #1	$434.00 every 6 mo.	$1181 per yr.	$39.55 per mo. and $56.00 per mo.
Agent #2	$396.41 every 6 mo.	$910.91 per yr.	$39.55 per mo. and $56.00 per mo.
Agent #3	$358.69 every 6 mo.	$1014.18 per yr.	$32.66 per mo and $42.92 per mo.
Agent #4	$475.29 every 6 mo.	$1537.33 per yr.	$34.30 per mo and $48.17 per mo.

As you can see, there are big differences in both auto and home insurance quotes, even though all agents represent the same company. The life insurance figures do not vary as much, but as you can see, Agent # 3 seems to have the best all-around rates.

Agents everywhere have the ability to charge as they see fit, over what the main companies charge them. Some are a little greedier than others. Some may have nicer offices or have to pay higher rents, and some may have more employees. Whatever the reason, you can not take for granted that any insurance provider or agent will be charging the same fees. Agent # 4 seems to be quite a bit more out of line than the other three agents. Always do your homework, even though it may take a little time out of your life. The money you will save will be well worth your while.

I know that it seems like all I mention are the problems in this country—and with good reason. Americans are so complacent, so willing to just accept things the way they are, that not enough gets done to address and repair these issues in this great land. If we can just find a way to work together and solve these problems, America would be a much nicer and cleaner place in which to live. It would be a land of people who truly care for one another, who look out for each other and are willing to help someone in need. There are people like that out there. I've met hundreds of them, but there are more people who are just not willing to get involved, for one reason or another.

Ever go to a town or city and see the homeless people on the streets? People standing on the corners begging for money! I have experienced this firsthand, time and time again for years. At first, I would drop a few dollars into their hands hoping to help them out. I have taken some into restaurants and fed them. But after seeing the same person day after day, year after year, on the same street corners begging, it got to be just plain annoying! I stopped one day and spoke with a regular guy whom I passed and helped out from time to time. I asked him why he didn't go and find employment. He told me that work was too hard and, besides, he could make more panhandling on the corners of the city in one day than he could make in a week at a regular job.

For me and others this problem with the homeless or street person had gotten so bad that when I went to work early in the morning, I had to step over or walk around these people sleeping on the sidewalks. Sometimes, I would park my car in a gated parking garage and find people sleeping in the stairwells. I don't know about you, but that can give me quite a start when I'm not expecting it. I can only imagine how a woman would feel when that happened to her. When I worked in the city, I would get in by 5:00 AM, and there were women I worked with who were coming in at the same time. I would ask these women to let me know where they were parking, just so I could walk them in safely. You never know what to expect, so it was my sense of duty as a man to be there for them, I felt. It's just the way I was raised.

I have heard on more than one occasion, though I have no real evidence to support this, that some cities give the homeless a one-way bus ticket to other cities just to get rid of them. I guess that's one way to do it. There has to be a better way. It costs the cities and the taxpayers a lot of money to deal with these homeless street people, not to mention all of the free food, shelter, clothing, and volunteer aid donated day after day to help those who could, in most cases, help themselves. Once again, something needs to be done. Laws need to be put in place that deter this type of behavior.

Some of these street-wise people who are just too lazy to work should be made to work for their meals and clothing. Put them to work cleaning the streets they love to live on in our cities. There are jobs all over the towns and cities we live in that might persuade them that maybe it's better to go get a real job. Get these people back in the game of life as productive citizens earning a living like the rest of us.

I am all for charity and have given to organizations like United Way for over thirty-three years. I volunteer locally, working with special needs children every week, so that they can have a better life. I also give at church. I donate to Goodwill, the Salvation Army, and countless others charities so that people in need can have some of life's necessities.

When I see street people who are capable of helping themselves begging, I see a need for real change. America must not ignore or turn a blind eye to this problem. The problem will not just go away, so we can't act like it doesn't affect us. It does affect us all, whether you're willing to admit it or not. Let's help these people find work and places to live. Cities need to set up rules for these homeless people and then enforce the rules. It's possible many of these homeless people could work for the city or town in which they choose to live. They can then receive life's necessities or else get a job—the choice is theirs. Then we will be able to redirect the kindness people have shown to these homeless street people to others whose needs are a bit more pressing, such as orphans, the disabled, single mothers, etc.

Most of the homeless people I've run into are in need of just a little understanding and direction. I have faith that if the American people would just pull together and volunteer some portion of their week, then changes can be made. Change is a good thing when it benefits us all and not just a few. Cleaning up society is just as important as cleaning up the air we breathe. It does not cost you anything but time to help out someone in need and, if you wish, go ahead and use some of your monetary resources. I think you will get a nice, warm feeling for your effort. It's called love!

Summary

Just to summarize what I have said: remember that the only way change will happen is if we all pull together.

Educating people is a key factor, especially in these uncertain times. Our grade schools need to take a different approach to educating the youth of America. Teaching finance, technology, teamwork, healthy lifestyles, and accountability will help with our children's futures and the future of America.

Our dependency on oil must be eliminated. Converting our cars and trucks to natural gas and the development of other sources like hydrogen and electric autos are a must.

The use of wind and solar power will play a big factor

in eliminating some of our dependency on oil, natural gas, and even coal.

Building both nuclear and pump storage electrical power plants is a must. They, too, will eliminate the need for any oil burning power plants, along with the reduction of natural gas and coal plant usage. America must demand that all utilities get on board if we are to succeed.

Taxes must be made fair for all, and the tax codes need to be easy to understand.

Illegal immigrants need to be held accountable, and rules that make sense, governing their rights in our country, need to be written and enforced.

Politicians and big business must find a way for insurance, the Social Security program, and Medicare to be equitable and affordable for all.

And, above all, our political leaders must be held accountable for their actions. They must campaign only with truth that can be substantiated.

The solution to all of the issues we face in America starts with you and your willingness to stand up and make a difference. Your opinions are a means to an end if you will only take things seriously and get involved. Live life as you would want it, with freedom and peace of mind, knowing you're part of the solution and not the problem.

A Final Thought ...

Let me leave you with one final thought regarding our past, as well as the future of our country. I remember when I was young and starting each school day. We did something that we all took for granted. I don't think they can even do this in school anymore. Each one of us stood up straight and proud, faced the flag, put our hands over our hearts, and took an oath. Remember?

I pledge allegiance to the flag of the United States of America and to the republic for which it stands, one nation under God with liberty and justice for all!

I ask all Americans to read those words and ask yourself what that pledge means to you. Can we regain the pride we once had when these words were so proudly repeated day after day, or are we destined for failure?

I know there is *hope* for America. I know there is still *love* in this country. We know we need *help!* It must come from us all. There is still *goodness* in America.

I believe these things with all my heart. God bless America!

Thank you. Have a wonderful life!